SPIT

WHAT'S COOL ABOUT DROOL

MARY BATTEN

FIREFLY BOOKS

To Filomène and Tatum
My precious grandchildren

A FIREFLY BOOK

Published by Firefly Books Ltd. 2019
Copyright © 2019 Firefly Books Ltd.
Text copyright © 2019 Mary Batten
Photographs © as listed on page 62

All rights reserved. No part of this publication may be
reproduced, stored in a retrieval system, or transmitted
in any form or by any means, electronic, mechanical,
photocopying, recording or otherwise, without the prior
written permission of the Publisher.

First printing

Library of Congress Control Number: 2019937618

Library and Archives Canada Cataloguing in Publication
Title: Spit : what's cool about drool / by Mary Batten.
Names: Batten, Mary, author.
Description: Includes index.
Identifiers: Canadiana 2019008829X | ISBN
9780228102267 (hardcover) | ISBN 9780228102328
(softcover)
Subjects: LCSH: Saliva—Juvenile literature. | LCSH:
Drooling—Juvenile literature.
Classification: LCC QP191 .B38 2019 | DDC
j612.3./13—dc23

Published in the United States by
Firefly Books (U.S.) Inc.
P.O. Box 1338, Ellicott Station
Buffalo, New York
14205

Published in Canada by
Firefly Books Ltd.
50 Staples Avenue, Unit 1
Richmond Hill, Ontario
L4B 0A7

Cover design: Hartley Millson
Interior design: Sam Tse
Illustrations: James Braithwaite

Printed in China

CONTENTS

WHAT'S COOL ABOUT DROOL?

Shut your mouth and swallow. It seems like no big deal, right? But you can only do this because your mouth is full of spit, or saliva. Without saliva, your tongue would stick to the roof of your mouth. You wouldn't be able to swallow, eat or talk. You would choke to death.

Outside your body, spit can seem like a nasty, slimy blob. But inside your mouth, it does some important things. It keeps your mouth moist. It starts digesting food the minute you take a bite. Its microbes help keep you from getting sick. Plus, just a tiny drop contains DNA, the molecule with the genetic blueprint that makes you YOU.

Spit is important for other animals too. Without spit, the cobra would have no venom, the chameleon wouldn't be able to catch its prey and the fly couldn't barf onto your hotdog and slurp up its meal. Plus, scientists are looking to spit for cutting-edge cures for everything from malaria to heart disease to cancer.

Turns out, spit is actually pretty incredible: who knew? So sit back and read on to find out more about how spit (or slobber, drool, saliva or whatever you like to call it) is actually the unsung hero of our time—or at least of our mouths.

CHAPTER 1

WHAT'S IN YOUR MOUTH?

"The mouth is one of the most biologically diverse worlds on the planet."

So says Dr. Douglas Granger, an American scientist who has been studying spit for many years. We think of biodiversity in rainforests and oceans — nature's ecosystems — but you have a diverse natural ecosystem right inside your mouth. It is a world of the small. Scientists call this world a *microbiome*.

INTRODUCING... The Microbiome

A microbiome is a community of microbes — tiny life forms that can only be seen with a microscope. The human microbiome lives mostly in our gut but is present throughout our bodies (including, of course, in our spit!).

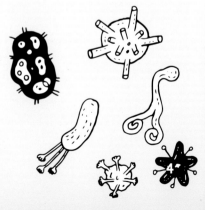

Although saliva is 99 percent water, the remaining one percent contains thousands of bacteria, viruses, proteins, enzymes, hormones, painkillers, natural antibiotic and antifungal substances, and DNA.

"Ew, all this nasty stuff in my mouth?" you might ask. Don't panic. Most of these components are actually mini-helpers! For instance, many bacteria and viruses are not bad. The few that cause disease get all the attention, but the ones in your mouth actually help keep you well.

Did you know that every day you produce about a quart (1 liter) of saliva? You begin producing it when you are born and continue throughout your life. Over the years, that adds up to a lot of drool!

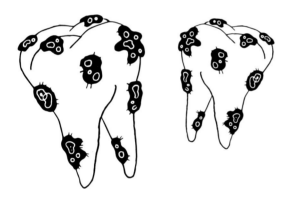

The Tiny Creatures Between Your Teeth

One of the first people to see bacteria in the mouth was 17th-century Dutch businessman and lens maker Antonie van Leeuwenhoek, who created microscopes so that he could examine the world in teeny-tiny detail. He looked at the plaque between his teeth and was amazed by what he saw.

NO AIR, NO PROBLEM

The little bugs in your spit are special. They don't need oxygen. The same air you breathe to stay alive would kill them. They are *anaerobes* — organisms that grow without air — which works perfectly, as your mouth doesn't have much oxygen because of all that liquid saliva!

Each year the average person produces enough saliva to fill two bathtubs.

In a letter written in 1683 to the Royal Society (a famous British scientific organization), he described the hidden world that his lens revealed:

I then most always saw, with great wonder, that in the solid matter there were many very little animalcules, very prettily a-moving. The biggest sort . . . had a very strong and swift motion, and shot through the water (or spittle) like a pike does through the water. The second sort . . . oft-times spun round like a top . . . and these were far more in number.

He called them *animalcules* because he thought they looked like tiny animals. Up until then, no one had known they existed.

Wondering whether the same little creatures were in other people's mouths, van Leeuwenhoek also looked at the plaque of two women — possibly his wife and daughter — and two old men who had never cleaned their teeth. In the mouth of one of the old men, he described "an unbelievably great company of living animalcules, a-swimming more nimbly than any I had ever seen up to this time . . . Moreover, the other animalcules were in such enormous numbers that all the water . . . seemed to be alive."

A PARTY IN YOUR MOUTH

HEY NERD! DO YOU MIND?
WE'RE TRYING TO HAVE A GOOD TIME IN HERE!

MORE ABOUT . . .
Van Leeuwenhoek

In the late 1600s, van Leeuwenhoek made simple handheld microscopes and began to examine all kinds of things, from lake water to plant cells to gunk from the human mouth. These gadgets were not like the microscopes you have at school today — they were really a kind of magnifying glass — but they revealed things people had never seen before. Van Leeuwenhoek was not a scientist, but he was curious and wanted to learn as much about the minute details of everything around him as he could.

By the time he died in 1723, he had made more than 500 optical lenses and at least 25 microscopes, some of which could magnify things up to 275 times — that's like making a fog droplet look like a basketball hoop. Compared with today's microscopes (which can magnify whatever you put in front of the lens to thousands of times its size), van Leeuwenhoek's instruments were crude, but at the time, they were high tech — and they allowed him to discover a world no one had previously known existed.

Many people made fun of van Leeuwenhoek and didn't believe he could possibly be seeing the things he was describing, but that didn't stop him. With the instinct of a scientist, he continued to describe everything he saw in his microscope with great detail. Since he couldn't draw well, he hired an artist to make pictures of his observations. For his work, van Leeuwenhoek became known as "the father of microbiology."

A replica of Van Leeuwenhoek's first microscope. The specimen was to be placed on the metal point and viewed through the tiny glass lens.

When van Leeuwenhoek found those creepy-crawlies, he didn't know that what he was seeing were bacteria. The word *bacteria* — a term meaning tiny, single-celled organisms that don't have a nucleus — wasn't introduced until 1838, more than 150 years after he first looked through his microscope. Bacteria can be bad (like the kinds that make you sick) or good (like the kinds that help you digest food), and either way, our bodies are home to trillions of them.

Bring on the Glands

Glands are organs that make substances your body needs. Some types (called exocrine glands) make stuff that comes out of you (like sweat and spit) and other types (called endocrine glands) make hormones that go into your bloodstream and help tell your body what to do. Special exocrine glands make saliva 24 hours a day. The largest of our saliva glands are the parotid glands that make almost a third of your body's saliva. The submandibular glands located under each jaw are the second-largest and produce the most saliva — up to 65 percent. The sublingual glands produce only 5 percent of the saliva in your mouth. Each of these glands transports saliva to your mouth via ducts (or tubes).

Each gland produces a different kind of saliva. The parotid glands produce watery saliva that helps in chewing — the first step in digestion. The submandibular and sublingual glands are called "mixed glands" because they produce both watery saliva and thick, gooey saliva containing mucus. Saliva from the sublingual glands is mostly mucus.

There are also hundreds of minor spit glands in your lips, tongue, cheeks, and sinuses, mouth and throat. Most of these are too small to be seen with the naked eye.

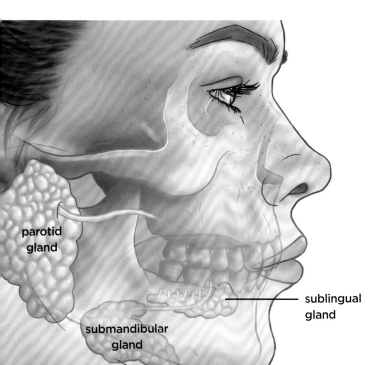

parotid gland

sublingual gland

submandibular gland

CHAPTER 2

CHEW, CHEW, CHEW

Snakes swallow their food whole. Humans, however, need to chew their food. It's the first step in digestion — using your teeth to crush and grind food into smaller and smaller bits that you can swallow. Muscles in your face move your jaws to help your teeth do the work.

You're not aware of it, but when you bite, your jaws chomp down at high pressure — around 70 pounds per square inch for your back teeth, depending on the kind of food. All this chomping could quickly wear away your teeth, but luckily, chewing triggers your glands to produce more spit, which protects your pearly whites. And that's a good thing, since you need them to last a lifetime!

In some cultures, mothers pre-chew food and feed it to their babies. This may sound gross, but it's good for the infant. A mother's saliva helps boost her baby's immune system. And it's not just for humans: other animal moms and dads pre-chew food for their babies too, including wolves, penguins and most other birds.

Wide World of Teeth

Each animal species has evolved teeth appropriate for the foods it eats:

- Carnivores, or meat-eaters, have pointy razor-sharp teeth for ripping, shredding and tearing their prey. Sharks have about 300 teeth arranged in many rows, but other carnivores, like lions, just have a single row (though they are still sharp!)
- Omnivores eat both plants and animals. In contrast to meat-eaters, omnivores have only eight cutting teeth, called incisors. Next to these are four sharp, pointy teeth called canines. The rest of the teeth are molars with flat surfaces for chewing and grinding food. Humans and apes are examples of omnivores.
- Herbivores eat only plants. Because of this they tend to have wide, flat molars for tackling fibrous plant material. As far back as millions of years ago, the vegetarian hadrosaurs had similar teeth. Their enormous mouths had over 600 giant molars so that they could eat tough foods like pine cones.

Carnivore

Omnivore

Herbivore

TO CLEAN AND PROTECT

If stomach acid built up in your mouth, it would wear away your tooth enamel. But, saliva to the rescue! Saliva is alkaline, which is the opposite of acid. This means it prevents acid from building up in your mouth and damaging your tooth enamel. Saliva also helps clean your mouth by flushing away food particles. It contains an enzyme that kills some bacteria. (But you still need to brush your teeth!) When you're asleep, you don't produce much saliva, so bacteria build up in your mouth, which can lead to "dragon breath" in the morning.

Ready to Eat

Even before you take a bite of that brownie, your salivary glands are getting your mouth ready to do its work by releasing spit. Your stomach is getting ready too. It's starting to produce the hydrochloric acid that helps you digest food.

But first, the enzymes in your saliva help dissolve the food into a form your body can use. Saliva also has another job: it lubricates and mixes with food to form a bolus — a small, slippery ball that you can swallow easily. It may sound unappetizing, but you could not swallow dry food, such as a cracker or a chip, unless saliva moistened and softened it first. Thanks, saliva!

AUTOMATIC? IT'S AUTONOMIC!

You don't have to think about producing spit. Your body does it automatically. Signals from your brain tell the salivary glands to do their thing. That's because they are connected to your autonomic, or involuntary, nervous system — of which your brain is the control center. This system also keeps you breathing and your heart pumping, without you giving it a second thought. All in a day's work for that brilliant brain!

 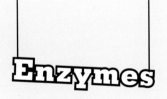

Enzymes are helper molecules (the scientific word is catalysts) that make chemical reactions happen. Our saliva contains digestive enzymes that help with — you guessed it! — digestion. One of the most important digestive enzymes is called amylase, which breaks down starchy foods such as grains, pasta and beans and changes the starch into simple sugars . . . right in your mouth! It also makes chocolate, ice cream and pudding taste even creamier — which is definitely a good thing.

MORE ABOUT . . .
Chewing, with Ruminants

If you were a cow, goat, giraffe, camel or other member of a group of animals called ruminants, you would chew, swallow your partially digested food and then regurgitate it back into your mouth and chew some more. Gross, right? Not really. Ruminants have to do this because the hay and other high-fiber plant food they eat is hard to digest. The secret to their digestion is lots of saliva and a special stomach that helps regurgitate their food.

After a cow, for instance, takes a bite, chews and swallows, its food goes into the first chamber of its stomach, called the rumen. Bacteria in the rumen soften and break down the food. Then this chamber's muscles send this semi-digested food (called the cud) back into the animal's mouth for more chewing. This can add up to some 30,000 chews a day! After the food is chewed for a second time, it is swallowed into the next part of the stomach, called the omasum. Believe it or not, there's one more stomach chamber to go, called the abomasum. Cows spend about eight hours a day chewing their cud, and as you'd expect, all this chewing releases a lot of saliva: 26 to 39 gallons (100 to 150 liters) a day! The saliva helps ferment the plant foods and also contains a natural antacid that protects the stomach (so it doesn't digest itself).

Luckily, people don't have to chew that much. But in order to get the most nutrients from our food, scientists say we should chew each mouthful 30 to 40 times. Besides being a cause of choking, not chewing food enough is as wasteful as pumping gasoline onto the ground instead of into your car's tank. Think of food as fuel for your body. Slow down and enjoy each tasty mouthful (and be thankful it's not hay).

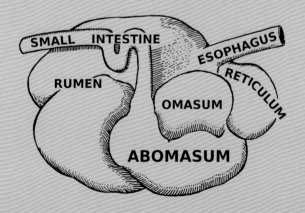

KINDS OF SPIT

Depending on whether your food is going down (when you're eating) or up (when you're barfing), there are five kinds of salivation:

- Cephalic — triggered by the sight or smell of something delicious, such as ice cream or freshly baked muffins.
- Buccal — triggered by food in the mouth, as you bite into that apple, hamburger, slice of pie, etc.
- Esophageal — triggered by food passing through the esophagus (the tube that connects the throat to the stomach).
- Gastric — triggered by some irritation in the stomach, such as contaminated food that gives you food poisoning and makes you vomit.
- Intestinal — triggered by food that doesn't agree with you passing through the upper intestine, making you vomit.

Taste First

Part of the pleasure of eating is tasting, but you wouldn't taste anything unless saliva dissolved the chemicals in your favorite foods. It's those chemicals that stimulate the thousands of taste buds on your tongue.

These buds (actually organs in their own right) send information to your brain so you instantly know whether the food in your mouth tastes sweet, salty, sour or bitter. A fifth taste called *umami*, a Japanese word, has recently been added to these four. It refers to a meaty taste, characteristic of beef broth.

Then Swallow

Once you've chewed and swallowed, food travels down your esophagus into your stomach, which is filled with hydrochloric acid. This acid is strong enough to dissolve metal. You might wonder why it doesn't dissolve your stomach too, but our bodies are quite marvelous. A coating of mucus protects the stomach lining.

A lot of action takes place in this amazing organ. Hydrochloric acid breaks down chewed food into even smaller particles of nutrients and other substances. These are then absorbed through your intestinal walls into your bloodstream, which carries nutrients to all parts of your body to rebuild cells and keep you healthy.

The Science of Dog Drool

Around 1890, Russian scientist Ivan Pavlov began studying digestion in dogs. He outfitted a group of dogs with tubes that could collect and measure their saliva. And every day, he and his assistants — in their matching white lab coats — would bring each dog a bowl of food. As the dogs began eating, their saliva flowed into the tubes.

One day, Pavlov noticed that the dogs began drooling when he merely walked into the room. Like any good scientist, he wondered what was going on. Eventually, Pavlov realized that the dogs had learned that people wearing white coats meant food was coming. Just the sight of the white coat triggered the drooling.

CHARLIE HAD SERVED THE ODD DOG IN HIS TIME,
BUT THE NEW WHITE LAB COATS CHANGED EVERYTHING.

MORE ABOUT . . .
Ivan Pavlov

Born in 1849, Ivan Pavlov was a Russian physiologist (a scientist who studies living things). He is best known for his experiments with dogs, proving that they could learn to associate food with other unrelated prompts. For instance, he would play a sound on a harmonium before feeding them and do this many times over. Eventually, the dogs would salivate whenever they heard the harmonium, knowing it meant food. Pavlov called these conditioned responses. He knew his theory related to people's behavior too. So if your mouth starts watering when you hear a friend open a chocolate wrapper, don't be embarrassed. Just tell them: it's Pavlovian.

He continued these experiments, showing that the animals could learn to associate many different triggers with food, like the sound of a buzzer or the clicking of a metronome. For the next 33 years, until his death in 1936, Pavlov devoted himself to understanding what was happening in the brains of these dogs. But his goal went further: he believed his work was important to understanding human behavior as well. And to think it all started with dog drool!

CHAPTER 3

YOUR SPIT IS YOU

Your spit is as individual as you are. The microbes in your mouth, which you develop when you are a baby, stay with you throughout your life. They are like fingerprints that can be used to identify you — and can even point to other members of your family. People in different countries have distinctive microbes too. But your saliva doesn't just tell who you are or where you came from. It has other biological markers that can help diagnose disease and other health conditions. Yes, that gooey liquid in your mouth speaks volumes about the secret that is you!

The Clues in Your Drool

In addition to microbes, your saliva also contains DNA, which carries genetic information that you inherited from your parents. Think of it as the blueprint for you, the material that makes you unique. It is the DNA in saliva that enables detectives to use it to solve crimes. Spit left on a glass, a cup, a phone or a toothbrush provides DNA.

Even dried spit on an envelope has enough DNA to tell who licked the seal. Beyond that, various companies even claim they can use spit to tell where people's ancestors came from — all the way back to caveperson days. But the jury's still out on whether these tests are accurate or just spitting in the wind.

INTRODUCING... DNA!

DNA stands for deoxyribonucleic acid — a molecule that contains all the instructions for how to make you the living, breathing person you are. It's present in almost every single cell of your body (including in your drool). There is no one else on Earth exactly like you, and your particular DNA is yours alone. It is the most personal information you have. Some people think it is so valuable that you shouldn't give it away without thinking carefully about how it may be used or abused.

ALWAYS WEAR THE BIB

When you go to the dentist and have your teeth cleaned, you usually produce a lot of spit. This is because the dental hygienist puts instruments in your mouth, and they trigger your salivary glands to produce more saliva. It's normal to drool a lot when your teeth are being cleaned. Fortunately, the hygienist has a handy suction tool (called a saliva ejector) to vacuum it out of your mouth, so all that spit doesn't get in the way while they polish up your pearly whites.

DR. PUNDERGROUT WAS AN EXPERT
IN THE "SPIT AND POLISH" TECHNIQUE.

Spit for Your Health

It's not just teeth dentists are experts in — it's also spit. It was dental researchers who pioneered saliva studies, starting with their interest in plaque on teeth (and all its microbes — shout-out to van Leeuwenhoek!). But saliva research has advanced far beyond dental plaque. Have you ever heard of a spit test? This isn't a test you study for in school — it's a medical test. But unlike a blood test, there are no needles and it doesn't hurt one bit. A nurse just swabs the inside of your cheek, or you spit into a cup or drool into a tube, and that's all there is to it. Then the spit sample goes to a laboratory where it's analyzed.

Dentists can use spit tests to find out who might develop cavities or gum disease. Doctors can use spit tests to tell if a person has diseases such as hepatitis C or HIV (the human immunodeficiency virus). Although the medical industry is developing these tests now, one day soon, they may replace some blood tests, which is a nice idea for those of us who don't enjoy the jab of a needle!

THERE'S A SPIT TEST FOR THAT?

Researchers are working on spit tests to detect heart disease, hormone imbalances and even brain damage from a concussion. Various kinds of cancer may leave markers in saliva as well. In the United States, the National Cancer Institute is funding a project to learn if saliva can be used to detect lung cancer at an early stage, when it is easier to treat. Who would have thought your drool could be a lifesaver?!

Spit for Sports

For an athlete, overexercising can be a real problem. It can stress the immune system, making the person more likely to get sick. And guess what can be used to determine stress by measuring an increase in certain hormones? That's right: saliva! Team doctors and coaches in England, Australia and several other countries use spit tests to tell how their athletes are doing. Some countries use these tests for their Olympic athletes too.

If the results show that someone has been exercising too hard, coaches can make changes in the training schedule to prevent sickness. There's even a portable device for when athletes are on the road. Right now, these tests are only available for top-level professional athletes, including swimmers, marathon runners and rugby and soccer players. Although they're not yet a routine

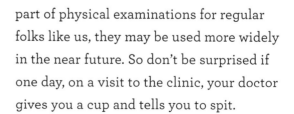

A doctor checks an athlete for a concussion. Soon, doctors may only need to ask athletes for their spit.

part of physical examinations for regular folks like us, they may be used more widely in the near future. So don't be surprised if one day, on a visit to the clinic, your doctor gives you a cup and tells you to spit.

CHAPTER 4

SPITTING HAPPY, SPITTING SCARED

ogs have spit. Cats have spit. Elephants have spit. Most animals have spit, and in the same way as it tells a lot about you, so it can tell a lot about these creatures. Just as with humans, stress in animals causes certain hormones to rise — which can be measured in their saliva. This is particularly important information for zoo veterinarians and keepers who want to ensure their animals are healthy and happy, and who want to help ease the stress for critters being moved from one zoo to another (because being the new zebra on the block isn't always easy).

INTRODUCING... STRESS!

Imagine a tiger suddenly appeared in front of you. You'd be terrified. You'd feel a surge of energy as your body prepared you to fight or get away. This reaction is called the "fight-or-flight" response. It's an inherited reaction from our ancient human ancestors who faced dangers from wild beasts. Although we don't usually face tigers these days, we do sometimes feel fearful and anxious in response to life's challenges; this is called stress. It produces a rush of the chemical adrenaline, causes an increase in our heart rate and changes enzyme and hormone levels in our bodies (including the stress hormone cortisol), which researchers can measure in our spit. Wondering if you're stressed out? Ask your spit!

Open Wide

Most zoo animals are trained to stand still and open wide so the zoo vet can check their teeth, gums and the general health of their mouth. Once the animals have learned this skill, researchers needing saliva samples just need to swab away. Spit tests are perfect for zoo animals. Blood tests are difficult to collect, and they're uncomfortable, just as they are for people. Collecting spit is minimally invasive and takes advantage of something the animal has already been trained to do. When the results of saliva tests are combined with observations of the animal's behavior, it is possible to tell whether the zoo has succeeded in creating habitats where the animals can live happily. And happy zoo animals are healthy zoo animals!

So how do you collect spit from a giant animal? First, you have to train it to open its mouth — which takes a lot of patience. Each time the animal opens up, the trainer gives it a reward, usually a favorite food. Polar bears open wide for meatballs, elephants for carrots, sweet potatoes or their favorite: alfalfa pellets that researchers call "elephant candy."

Once that part is done, you just need the right swab for the job. For elephants, it takes a swab about the length of a pencil. But the researchers can't just stick their arms in the elephants' mouths! The swab has to be attached to a long handle (plastic rods normally used to open and close blinds work nicely). For gorillas, the device is similar, but the swab is made of super-absorbent dental gauze that the animals chew on, depositing a lot of their spit for lab technicians to analyze. Drool acquired!

Time for Love

Zoos all over the world use spit tests not only to tell whether their animals are happy, but also to learn the best time to put a male and female together to breed. For instance, scientists at a zoo in Mexico collected spit from hippos to find out when the females were ready to mate. First, the hippos had to be trained to walk into a chute and drop their bottom jaw. Then researchers were able to collect their saliva with a paper cup. (They said the spit poured out of the hippos' saliva glands like a water fountain. Gross!)

If the mating is successful, saliva can also be used for a pregnancy test. African black rhinos are so large that it's impossible to tell when females are pregnant just by looking, so spit tests are the only way to know if they have a little rhino on the way. Many zoos are saving endangered animals from extinction through breeding programs, making these spit tests potential species-savers.

THE OLD STRESS TEST

JIMMY HADN'T EXPECTED THE POP QUIZ
IN COCKROACH HISTORY.

INSECTS FEEL STRESS TOO

What could possibly stress a cockroach? They outlasted the dinosaurs and are hundreds of millions of years old. But scientists who study roaches say they make spit bubbles when they're subjected to stress — such as when they're picked up. (Being handled by a primate thousands of times larger than you would be understandably jarring.) Some roaches also have pheromones — scents — in their spit to communicate danger and to attract other roaches of their species. Kind of makes you appreciate the lowly cockroach, doesn't it? Or maybe not.

Panicked Puppies

Think of the scariest thing you can imagine. If you were a dog, that might be a thunderstorm. Many a dog owner has come home from work to find her home wrecked — furniture overturned, upholstery torn up and bite marks on the woodwork. At least one terrified dog has jumped through a plate-glass window in fear. Thunder makes some dogs go into full panic mode.

To find out just how stressful thunderstorms are for dogs, a research veterinarian set up an experiment. She played loud recordings of thunderstorms and collected spit from a group of dogs. When the dogs heard the thunder, they panted, paced, whined and drooled. Levels of the stress hormone cortisol (as measured in their saliva) increased more than 200 times and stayed high for a long time, up to 40 minutes after the test. Some dogs were so scared they needed medicine to calm down. After the experiment was over, the researcher recommended that dog owners provide a safe place, such as a covered crate or a basement, where their pets could go during a storm. That could help Rover feel more safe and secure . . . and save on home repair costs.

Therapy Dogs

Dogs are smart, sensitive animals with an amazing ability to bond with people. They can even help improve our health. A Canadian study was done with a group of children who had autism spectrum disorder (ASD, a condition that can cause trouble with communicating, difficulty with social interactions and sensory overload). Anxiety is also a part of ASD, and these children had high levels of the stress hormone cortisol in their saliva on waking in the morning. But when their families were given therapy dogs, over time, something amazing happened: the level of cortisol decreased. Having these dogs by their sides helped reduce the kids' stress (and provided a warm, soft buddy too)! Grown-ups can also benefit from therapy dogs. An American study has shown that therapy dogs help veterans suffering from post-traumatic stress disorder (PTSD). It's a scientific fact: dogs really are people's best friends.

CHAPTER 5

THE BETTER TO EAT YOU, MY DEAR

Saliva helps everybody digest food, but spit helps some animals *catch* it too. For creatures such as frogs, it can trap and stun prey, and for animals that feed on blood like the vampire bat, it can keep the victim's blood flowing while they feast. Some bugs, like mosquitoes, also rely on saliva to help them chow down — though in their case, sometimes we wish it wasn't quite so successful.

The spitting spider is one of the fastest spitters in the animal kingdom. In 1/700th of a second, it spits venomous bands of gluey silk that form a net around its prey, trapping it. While the prey struggles to escape, the spider paralyzes it with venom. The spider's saliva turns the prey's insides into a mush that the spider sucks out. To have all this saliva at the ready, these spiders need two stomachs: one that holds silk for web-building and the other that holds their sticky spit.

Super Fast, Super Sticky

Faster than a racing car, stickier than superglue, able to connect in a single strike, the chameleon's tongue is a marvel of nature. When it sights a fly, cricket or other favorite prey, the chameleon shoots out its tongue, latches onto the critter and whips it back into its mouth just as fast. This extraordinary tongue, which is twice as long as the chameleon's entire body, catches the insect with — what else? — its spit. Chameleon spit is about 400 times stickier than a person's saliva. That's about as thick as honey. Their super-sticky spit enables chameleons to catch large prey that are up to a third of their body weight.

ONE SMALL SLURP FOR MANKIND

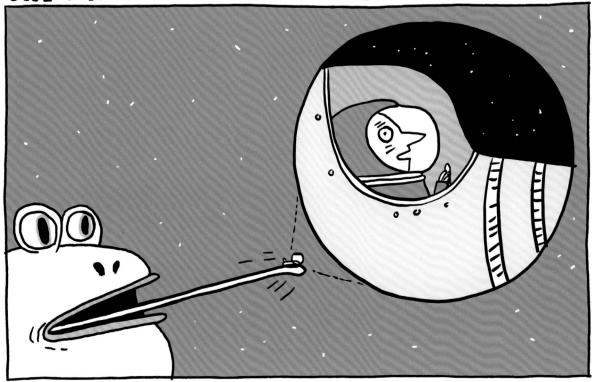

ALTHOUGH HE KNEW A FROG TONGUE IS FASTER THAN A
ROCKET LAUNCH, BUZZ WAS STILL UNPREPARED FOR THIS RIDE.

FROG TONGUE VERSUS ROCKET

Frogs have a speedy tongue, which shoots out five times faster than the blink
of an eye to capture an insect. Glued to the frog's tongue by saliva, the insect
is in for a fast ride back to the frog's mouth. Scientists have measured the
speed and have reported that it can reach 12 times the acceleration of gravity;
for comparison, astronauts usually experience three times the acceleration of
gravity when rocketing into space. Pretty impressive, frog tongue.

Fly Barf

You do not want to invite a housefly to a picnic. Its table manners are gross. It walks on its food because it tastes through its feet. And because a fly can't bite or chew, it has to use the bristles on the end of its proboscis (sucking tube) to break the food into tiny particles. Then it vomits a mixture of saliva and digestive juices onto the meal. Yuck. Fly barf makes the food liquid so the insect can use its mouthparts like a sponge to soak up the feast and deposit it into its stomach. All this to say that a fly's saliva is essential to its survival . . . and if you eat outdoors in the summer, you've definitely eaten some fly barf.

Buzzzz, Buzzzz

Annoying as they are, mosquitoes are interesting insects. They are the only creatures that can suck and spit at the same time. These pesky fliers, whose earliest ancestor dined on dinosaur blood, have complicated mouthparts, but only the female of the species feeds on blood. When a female mosquito bites, she uses a tiny needlelike mouthpart to inject saliva into her victim and a tubelike mouthpart to suck its blood right into her gut.

Mosquito spit contains a substance called an inhibitor that keeps the victim's blood from clotting so that it flows freely, enabling the mosquito to get a good meal. The saliva substances left under the skin cause an allergic reaction that you feel as an itchy bump. The more you scratch, the more it itches because you're spreading these substances around. So tempting as it may be, don't touch that bite!

Freeze! It's Shrew Venom

The tiny North American short-tailed shrew paralyzes its prey with spit. One of the few venomous mammals, this mouse-sized mole-like creature, makes venom in salivary glands located on each side of its throat. When it wants a meal, the shrew hunts insects, grubs and larvae, with the occasional baby bird, mouse and frog thrown in. Shrew venom doesn't kill the prey but paralyzes it, keeping it from getting away. This way, even if the shrew can't eat it right away, the fresh meal is there waiting for it.

FLYING DRACULA'S GROOVY TONGUE

Vampire bat saliva contains an enzyme that keeps its victim's blood flowing so the bat can feed. But the bat doesn't suck blood. It laps it up through grooves in its tongue. The South American vampire bat with the long name, *Desmodus rotundus*, which means "fat bat," drinks about two tablespoons of blood each night and shares blood with its young and other adult bats. How very generous!

Assassins in Our Midst

Assassin bugs ambush their prey, spear them with their beak and then feast on their fluids! The beaks of assassin bugs contain two tubelike mouthparts. One injects the victim with venomous saliva that paralyzes the prey and turns its body into mush. The other mouthpart acts as a straw, sucking the liquid into the bug's stomach. Yum, yum. In all, there are about 7,000 of these insects. Let's drag a few into the spotlight:

Kissing Bug

- The red spot assassin bug of Central Africa loves to dine on rhinoceros beetles. It is known as the least aggressive of these bugs.

- The wheel bug, one of the largest insects in North America — up to 1.5 inches (3.8 cm) in length — is another type of assassin bug. It's called the gardener's friend because it preys on caterpillars, beetles and other insects that eat plants and destroy crops. Glad it's on our side!

- The kissing bug earned the name because it often bites people's faces and lips. Found in the United States and Central and South America, this bug's bite packs a wallop. Not only does it hurt, but some people are allergic to its saliva (so the bite gets red and swollen). Worse, its poop can even cause an illness called Chagas disease. Don't let the sweet sounding nickname fool you, this bug's a nasty one!

CHAPTER 6

SPITTING FOR DEFENSE

Grab your goggles, cover your eyes and stay out of range of spit fire. Human saliva may not have any poisonous power, but spit is a dangerous weapon for some animals. Llamas, grasshoppers, venomous snakes and other critters defend themselves with it. From the venom of a cobra to the stinky spit of the llama to the barf of a grasshopper, this spit is crucial to these creatures for keeping trouble at bay. You know what they say: survival of the spittest!

INTRODUCING...

Venomous vs. Poisonous

Venomous animals deliver their toxin (a substance that can hurt or kill) by injecting it into their victims with fangs, teeth, spines or stingers. Poisonous animals, such as poison dart frogs and monarch butterflies, don't deliver their toxins directly; they have them in their bodies and must be eaten or touched by other animals in order for the toxins to do their work. So the difference is all in the delivery!

A Snake in the Grass

Snake venom (a type of saliva) is a toxin that snakes inject into their victims. They deliver their toxin through fangs, which are really hollow teeth that act like hypodermic needles. The toxin is produced in salivary glands behind the snakes' eyes. Among the most venomous snakes are sea snakes, adders, cobras and rattlesnakes. Depending on the species, getting bitten can cause swelling, blindness, convulsions, muscle spasms, kidney failure, shock, vomiting and death. Yikes. To be fair, only certain types of snakes are venomous . . . but it's no wonder people are spooked by these slithery critters!

Bush Viper

SNAKES BY THE NUMBERS

According to the World Health Organization, between 81,000 and 138,000 people die of snakebites every year. Most of these deaths occur in Africa, Asia and Latin America.

- More than 400,000 people suffer amputations and other permanent disabilities as a result of snakebite.
- Of the more than 3,000 species of snakes in the world, only about 600 are venomous. Some 200 of these are "medically important," meaning their bite can cause serious injury or death.
- North America has 160 species of snakes, but only about 20 of these are venomous.

Even though the likelihood of getting bitten is low (about 1 in 40,000), get to know which snakes are venomous where you live. And if you do see one, remember: it's more scared of you than you are of it. Move slowly, give it an escape route, and with any luck, it'll vamoose.

Firing from the Fangs

Spitting cobras don't really spit but contract their head and neck muscles, squeezing their venom glands. This forces a stream of venom from the fangs aimed at the face and eyes of predators. Keep your distance if you see one; these snakes are sharpshooters and can spray their venom as far as 6 feet (2 meters). They aim for the eyes and can hit their targets accurately. If venom hits the eyes, it can cause intense pain and even blindness. Keepers and vets who work with spitting cobras in zoos wear goggles and full face protection. Even baby spitting cobras have venom ready to fire as soon as they hatch.

King of the Snakes

Cobras, known for their trademark "hooded" appearance, are native to Asia and Africa. The king cobra is the largest venomous snake in the world, reaching a length of 18 feet (5.5 meters) and weighing up to 19.8 pounds (9 kilograms). Although it doesn't have the most toxic venom, because of its large size, it can inject more venom in a single bite than most other snakes. Its venom contains a powerful neurotoxin that causes paralysis, respiratory failure and death. A bite from a king cobra can kill a person in 15 minutes and a full-grown elephant in a

King Cobra

few hours. This snake eats other snakes, including other venomous species such as cobras and kraits. They don't call it the king for nothing.

THE QUICKEST SPIT IN THE WEST.

HE SAYS HE'S THE BEST SHARPSHOOTER ALIVE,
BUT IT'S THE COBRAS THAT DO ALL THE WORK.

INTRODUCING... 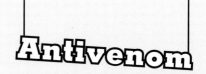 Antivenom

As you read these chilling descriptions of what snake venom can do to its victims, you might be thinking: But surely there's a medicine that can help? And indeed there is. In many countries, researchers "milk" venom from poisonous snakes to use in making something called antivenom (also called antivenin). The milking is (of course) difficult, and the process of making the antivenom is time consuming, but the results are a medication that can be used to save the lives of people suffering from snakebites—so it's well worth it!

Spitdown in the Desert

Living in the deserts of the southwestern United States and northwestern Mexico, the Gila (pronounced hee-la) monster is one of the few venomous lizards in the world. Old tales painted it as a fearsome creature that spit venom, had poisonous breath and boasted a bite that was fatal to humans. But in reality, this animal is slow and passive, its breath unremarkable and it mainly uses its venomous saliva for defense. If any animal, such as a coyote or bird of prey, threatens it, the Gila monster opens its mouth and hisses, a signal that says, "Back off!" If the attacker doesn't leave, the Gila monster bites with its sharp teeth and powerful jaws. It may stay locked on to the predator for up to 15 minutes, gnawing on its flesh and not letting go. This gnawing causes the Gila monster's venom to flow from its salivary glands through grooves in its teeth into the predator's bloodstream, hurting the creature enough that it backs off . . . or dies. Fortunately this venom isn't toxic to humans (though the bite is said to be excruciating).

THE GRASSHOPPER'S DEFENSE

If you pick up a grasshopper, you may get barfed on. Grasshoppers spit at predators, such as ants or humans who pick them up, to defend themselves. People call grasshopper spit "tobacco juice" because it looks like spit from people who chew tobacco, but, in fact, it is a combination of digestive juices and grasses and weeds that the critters eat.

Playing Possum

When opossums are very scared, they play dead. They fall over, body stiff and mouth open, baring sharp teeth. Fear also makes them produce a lot of spit, and drool drips from their mouths. This display makes predators think the opossum is dead and not fit to eat. Then, when the predator has moved on and it's safe again, the opossum comes to and goes on about its day (or night). It's an opossum miracle!

ONE, TWO, THREE TIMES A LLAMA

Llamas spit at each other to defend their food, and they'll spit at you or anything else that bothers them. You don't want to be the target of a spitting llama. They have three ways to spit at you, and none of them is pleasant:

- Spitting air and saliva into a mist, as a warning
- Spitting the food from their mouth (if they're eating)
- Spitting the contents of their stomach — which will be green, smell like barf and not wash off easily.

In short, don't irritate a llama. And if you do, take cover.

Adorable and Deadly

The slow loris, a big-eyed tree-dweller that lives in Southeast Asia, is the only venomous primate. And unlike the other venomous creatures thus far, it gets its venom through grooming. A gland inside each elbow secretes a stinky substance that gets into the animal's mouth as it licks itself. When the gland secretion mixes with saliva, it becomes toxic. As the name says, the loris is a slow-moving creature, so it needs all the help it can get to protect itself from predators. When threatened, the loris delivers its venom through a bite, which can cause the victim to go into shock, an extreme allergic reaction. The loris can also apply the toxic spit to the top of its head and the heads of its young, and the gross-smelling stuff is often enough to make the predator turn tail and choose a different meal. Toxic *and* stinky: the perfect combination.

CHAPTER 7

LICKETY SPIT: HEALING WITH SPIT

Have you ever bitten your tongue or the inside of your cheek? Ouch! Although it hurts, a mouth wound almost never gets infected, and it heals ten times faster than wounds on other parts of your body. That's because our spit has healing properties. And it's not just us — other animals seem to know instinctively that spit can heal. When a dog is hurt, for example, the first thing it does is lick its wounds. Science is on to saliva's medicinal possibilities, whether it be from shrews, leeches, mosquitoes or humans — and researchers throughout the world are working hard to learn everything they can about how they can use it to improve human health. When cutting-edge science meets drool . . . anything is possible!

WHAT'S IN HUMAN SPIT?

Human spit contains antifungal, antibacterial and antiviral substances. This means that it can prevent bad stuff like fungus, viruses and bacteria from thriving. Our spit also contains natural painkillers. One of them — opiorphin — is six times more powerful than morphine. All of this is good news for our mouths. It makes healing quicker and less painful. Scientists wonder: Could saliva also help heal wounds in other parts of the body? Research to answer this question is in very early stages, but one thing's for certain: there is plenty of potential in our miraculous spit.

Mosquitoes: The Bad

Mosquitoes aren't just annoying pests. They can carry everything from malaria, Zika virus, West Nile virus and dengue fever in their saliva — and they transfer that disease to whatever other animals they happen to bite, including humans. Because of how readily mosquitoes spread sickness, some have called them the most dangerous animal on Earth.

Instead of trying to develop a vaccine against each virus that mosquitoes carry, scientists are trying to make a universal vaccine that will trigger the body's immune response against mosquito spit. They discovered proteins in the saliva that form the basis of the vaccine, which is currently being tested in clinical trials. If it is successful, this medicine will prevent infection when a person is bitten. Researchers are hopeful that it will prevent future breakouts of a range of mosquito-borne diseases. Here's to humans fighting back against this buzzing bloodsucker!

The ancient Greeks and Romans had many superstitions about spit. They believed spit could prevent skin eruptions and cure snakebites, leprosy, eye inflammation and cancer. They also believed spitting could keep evil away, which probably led to the custom of spitting for luck.

INTRODUCING... Clinical Trials

It takes many years and lots of money to develop a vaccine — a medicine that can protect people against disease. Before it can become available to the general public, scientists first do test-tube experiments and tests on animals. If these tests show that the drug is safe, the researchers design clinical trials — research studies in which people participate. The people are usually divided into three groups: one takes the medicine being tested, ➡

the second receives the medicine plus something to boost its effectiveness and the third receives a dummy medicine called a placebo. At the end of the trial, the investigators examine the results to see which group had the best outcome. If the medicine worked, it's one step closer to being approved as a vaccine, a new tool to help us thwart disease.

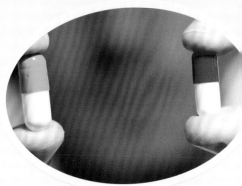

Mosquitoes: The Good

Normally, if you cut yourself, your blood clots to stop the bleeding; a scab forms, sealing the wound, and healing begins. This process is called hemostasis. "Hem" means blood and "stasis" means stopping. But when a mosquito bites, certain substances in its saliva prevent clotting and keep the victim's blood flowing so the insect can feed nonstop. These anticlotting substances may also be useful to us. Researchers have developed a clot-busting drug from mosquito saliva that might be used to treat blood clots that can lead to strokes or pulmonary thrombosis (when a clot gets to the lungs, which can be fatal). Good to know these little blood suckers have a positive side.

A different drug based on mosquito spit helps treat lung problems such as pneumonia and chest colds. An enzyme in the insect's saliva is capable of breaking down secretions in our airways and improves air flow to the lungs.

Thanks to the pesky mosquito, patients with these ailments can take a deep breath.

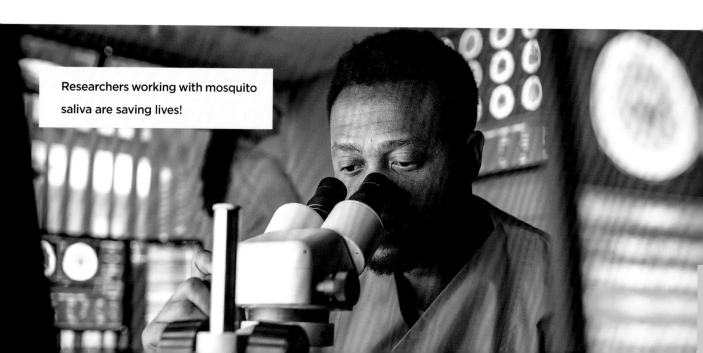

Researchers working with mosquito saliva are saving lives!

STICK AROUND, BUDDY!

SPIT GLUE: THE RELAXED TICK'S BEST FRIEND.

Tick Spit: Three Ways

1. GLUE: Ticks are parasites, meaning they live in or on other animals. When a tick finds a host, such as a dog or a person, it attaches itself to the skin with a kind of glue from its spit. Scientists think the tick's sticky saliva could possibly be used in a medical glue to help seal wounds and anchor torn ligaments and tendons to bone.

2. BLOOD THINNER: After ticks attach themselves, they feed on the host's blood, injecting saliva at the same time. A tick's saliva contains substances to keep the blood from clotting so the tick can feed.

Researchers are studying whether these anticlotting agents can be used to prevent tumors, break up blood clots and treat heart disease.

3. ANTI-INFLAMMATORY: Tick spit also has proteins that prevent inflammation (swelling), allowing the tick to stay in place 8 to 10 days without being noticed. Already a drug derived from one of these proteins has been shown to reduce inflammation in monkeys infected with SIV, the primate form of HIV. Someday this drug might help humans too!

UNSTICK THE TICK!

The spit of some ticks carries bacteria, viruses and parasites that cause serious illnesses such as Lyme disease — so if you find a tick on your body, you'll want to get it off as soon as possible. You may need a grown-up's help in removing it. Never try to scratch it off or remove it with your fingers — you need to remove the whole tick. Use tweezers to grasp the tick's entire body and pull it out, then clean the area and your hands with rubbing alcohol or soap and water. And remember: if you're wandering in tall grasses or woods, wear long pants and sleeves — and good bug repellent — to foil those tricky ticks before they take a bite!

Lovely Leeches

Many of the more than 1,000 species of leeches live in freshwater environments, such as rivers, ponds and lakes. These bloodsucking worms aren't anyone's favorite creature, because people often run into them while taking a summer's dip only to emerge from the water to find one (or several) attached to their skin. The leech has three jaws, which allow it to hold on to humans and other vertebrates (creatures with backbones) and suck their blood. When the leech bites, it injects saliva into the wound, which keeps the blood flowing so it can feed. Ick, right? But don't write them off entirely. Substances in leech saliva have anticlotting and anti-inflammatory properties, and scientists have discovered more than 100 components that can help in treating heart disease, diabetes, high blood pressure, inflammation and arthritis. Leech saliva may also contain anticancer substances. So perhaps we can take this moment to honor the leech's contribution to medical science . . . while insisting that they keep out of our local swimming hole.

LEECH HEALING IN HISTORY

Ancient Egyptian, Indian, Greek and Arab doctors used leeches to treat everything from skin diseases to dental problems, seizures to fevers. These ancient doctors believed disease was caused by impure blood. They thought that by using bloodsucking leeches to remove the troublesome blood, the body would heal. This treatment was called "bloodletting." Unfortunately for those patients in ancient times, losing that blood didn't really cure anything and only tended to make them sicker. Leeches stopped being prescribed that way in the 19th century, but they continue to be useful in medicine now. Ah, leeches: can't live with 'em, can't live without 'em.

Taming the Shrew

Short-tailed shrews have the distinction of being the only venomous mammal in North America. They inject their venom through their bite, using it to paralyze their prey. But this venom isn't just helpful to the shrew. It turns out that it contains a protein that scientists have developed into a medicine to help manage pain and possibly stop the growth of tumor cells in various cancers, including ovarian, breast, prostate, lung and pancreatic. Right now this drug is only available to patients participating in clinical trials, but researchers are working to make it more widely available in the future. Long live the shrew!

CHAPTER 8

COURTING WITH SPIT

You might not think spit could have anything to do with courtship. But it does. Think about us humans: kissing mouth to mouth — the romantic kind — is really an exchange of spit. You're probably saying "Yuck" right now. Kissing is gross if you only think about the spit part. But when love is involved, many people don't hesitate to pucker up and lock lips. Other creatures use spit in their courtships too, like bats, flies and bowerbirds. These creatures use it in different, more creative ways, like making spitball presents or mixing it into a stinky (but alluring) perfume. To each their own!

The Kiss Around the World

Kissing has been part of the human mating game in Western cultures for thousands of years, though some say the act originated in India and spread from there. Lips are 100 to 200 times more sensitive than the fingertips, which might explain why people would be inclined to press them together, and kissing helps people choose a mate. But kissing is not universal. Anthropologists — scientists who study people — found that more than half of the 168 human cultures they surveyed don't practice mouth-to-mouth

kissing. In some cultures, it was totally unknown. For those who do engage in smooching, they're not just being romantic — they're boosting their immune systems.

The exchange of bacteria, hormones and other substances from each person's saliva improves the kissers' microbiomes and helps them fight off infection. Kiss for your health!

Kissing Cousins

Our closest kin in the animal kingdom are chimpanzees and bonobos. We share about 99 percent of our DNA with these primates. Chimps (see below) and bonobos are the only other animals that kiss as we do — mouth to mouth. But kissing among chimps has nothing to do with romance. It's usually two males making up after a fight. Bonobos are more affectionate. They kiss a lot. Sometimes it has to do with bonobo love and sometimes with greeting friends. Whenever two animals kiss mouth to mouth, they exchange saliva. As with humans, hormones and other substances in the spit may enhance immunity and solidify bonds between the kissers. Nice to know these great apes know the power of a smooch.

SMELL YOU LATER

A LITTLE SPRITZ GOES A LONG WAY.

WING BAG COLOGNE

Among greater sac-winged bats, which live in the rainforests of Central and South America, females choose mates for their smell. Male bats have two small skin bags on their wings. Every day they spend up to an hour cleaning and filling the bags with a cocktail of saliva, urine and other secretions. Each male has his own individual smell. The bat's body heat causes the liquid to ferment, giving off a strong fragrance. When a male courts a female, he hovers in front of her, opens his wing bags and fans his perfume toward her. If she likes his odor, she allows him to mate. If not, he's out of luck.

Saliva Snack

The male scorpionfly is a champion spitballer. When he is courting a female, he must first present her with a spitball. And it better be a big one. Females prefer males with the largest gifts, and it's to the male's advantage to make the largest spitball he can. Females feed on the spitball, and mating lasts only as long as she's eating — so fast food is not to the male's advantage. Well-fed, healthy males have enlarged salivary glands and can produce more and larger spitballs than males in poor condition. Instead of spitballs, these less healthy males may catch an insect and offer it to females they're trying to woo. If the gift isn't to a female's liking, the male may steal it back and fly off to offer it to another female. Easy come, easy go.

THE ART OF SALIVA

To attract females, male bowerbirds build a fancy structure called a bower. They fashion it out of twigs and gathered objects, like flowers, sparkly rocks and berries. To add that extra finesse, certain types of bowerbirds will paint the bower with a mix of vegetable juices, charcoal and saliva to give their sculpture just the right tint. As they're waiting for a mate, they will continue to add touch-ups to keep their creation looking tip-top. These birds really know décor!

Bubble Wrap

Male dance flies, also called balloon flies, come courting with a tiny insect neatly wrapped. Some males wrap their gift in silk produced by glands on their front feet. But not all males make silk, so some wrap their gift in a frothy spit balloon. Then there are the tricksters that don't bother to spend their energy hunting down an insect. These guys just offer an empty spit balloon. The female doesn't know she's been tricked until she bites into the froth. Imagine the disappointment!

CHAPTER 9

THE MEANING OF SPIT

Spit is a pretty personal substance. It's produced in the privacy of our mouths, and we usually keep it to ourselves. It's an innate part of us, like our blood or our sweat. Perhaps this is why spitting — when some of that precious saliva lands outside of our bodies — has taken on so much significance in cultures around the world. It can be considered lucky, as with the custom of spitting over your left shoulder three times (the Russian equivalent of knocking on wood). Or it can be considered insulting, such as when someone spits at or near someone else. It can also just be part of tradition, such as in the world of baseball. No matter what, each culture has its own way of defining what spit means — good, bad and just . . . odd (we're looking at you, Pliny the Elder).

Very Super-spit-tious

Throughout history, people have believed that spitting on certain objects would ensure good fortune. Nobody knows why. Here are a few examples:

- ON THE WATER: Sailors spit in the ocean for luck on their voyages. Fishermen spit over the edges of their boats in hopes they'll have a good catch.

- IN BOXING: Historically, before a bare-knuckle match, fighters believed that spitting on their fists would make their blows more powerful. Today some boxers still spit on their gloves in hopes it will sway the fight their way.

- IN BASEBALL: Another still-practiced tradition is baseball players spitting on a new bat — or spitting into their hands before going up to bat — to ensure they'll play well.

- HORSESHOES: Irish folklore dictates that if you find a horseshoe, you should spit on it and then toss it over your shoulder for good luck. Not that you're so likely to run across a horseshoe these days . . .

SPIT AS SNAKE REPELLENT?

Pliny the Elder, a first-century Roman author, wrote an encyclopedia of 37 volumes called *Natural History.* This work influenced scientific and medical theories in Europe for more than 1,000 years. However, some of the things he said were based more on superstition than on fact. In one section, Pliny wrote:

> "**All men possess in their bodies a poison which acts upon serpents, and the human saliva, it is said, makes them take flight, as though they had been touched with boiling water. The same substance, it is said, destroys them the moment it enters their throat, and more particularly so, if it should happen to be the saliva of a man who is fasting.**"

So human spit terrifies snakes and can poison them? Here's hoping no one took Pliny's word on that . . .

Gobs of Protection

Many cultures also believe in the idea of bad luck, and in particular, the curse of the "evil eye," which can befall someone if they're given a particularly nasty glare, for instance. Being complimented or bragging can also invoke the evil eye because you are trying to set yourself above others, which is asking for trouble. The evil eye can be used to explain someone's misfortunes, especially if they have a string of bad luck or ill health. But good news is many cultures also believe that if you spit, you can ward off that curse. You don't have to actually shower anyone with saliva — just the act of saying "ptooey, ptooey, ptooey" (or some variation) gets across that you're spitting. People think that this might be because spitting is a form of sacrifice, which overcomes the bad vibes of the evil eye. You can spit to that!

Designated Spitters

Watch a baseball game and you'll see players — and coaches too — spitting. More than athletes in any other sport, baseball players spit. They developed the habit during the years when chewing tobacco was common — and players using it would have to spit out the tobacco juices every now and again. Today, all tobacco use is banned in major-league games, but players have other things to keep them expectorating: managers provide buckets of snacks in the dugout, so players will chew gum or eat candy or sunflower seeds. And then they'll spit. It's a tradition, something baseball aficionados consider a part of the game. Why exactly? Sometimes traditions are kept up just for tradition's sake. It wouldn't be baseball without 'em.

NATIONAL PASTIME

CODY CAN'T CATCH OR HIT, BUT HE'S THE BEST DESIGNATED SUNFLOWER SPITTER IN BASEBALL.

SPIT CAN CHANGE A PITCH?

Some baseball pitchers were famous for throwing spitballs. The spitball, also called a "spitter," got its name from the pitcher's habit of doctoring the ball with his spit or some other substance, such as petroleum jelly. If the pitcher put the ball in his mitt and then coughed on it or licked it, this changed the weight on one side and made it move in an unusual way. It was almost impossible to hit. Spitballs were officially banned in 1920, but some older pitchers who had been throwing them were allowed to keep doing so until they retired. Today's baseball rules say that if a pitcher touches his mouth with his pitching hand while on the plate or mound, he must wipe off his fingers before gripping the ball. If the pitcher violates this rule, the umpire calls the pitch a ball (as in, a bad pitch that counts against the pitcher). Keep that pitching hand dry!

MORE ABOUT . . . Preacher Roe

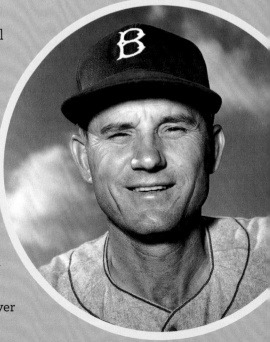

One of the most famous spitballers was Preacher Roe, whose real name was Elwin Charles Roe. A left-handed pitcher, he played for the Brooklyn Dodgers during the late 1940s and '50s when the spitball was illegal, but that didn't keep him from throwing them. After he retired in 1955, he explained how he put the spit on the ball. In an article for *Sports Illustrated* magazine, Roe said he wiped his left hand across his brow and spit on his thumb with juice from the bubble gum he was chewing. He used the base of his hand to hide what he was doing. Then while hitching up his belt, he wet his index and middle fingers, gripped the ball on a smooth spot and threw with a fastball motion. "I try to keep the hitters off balance, never giving them a decent pitch," Roe said. "I'm always aiming for the corners, never throwing the same pitch twice or what the hitter is expecting."

The Insult of Spit

Even though spitting can be handy in certain scenarios, it's all about the context. Spitting near or at someone . . . well, that's a no-no. Ask the soccer world! Tempers sometimes heat up on the soccer field, and one player will lob a gob at another. It's the most insulting thing a player can do. A tiff that made the news took place during the 1990 World Cup contest between Holland and Germany. Dutch player Frank Rijkaard spat into the hair of German player Rudi Völler.

The German press, angered by Rijkaard's slight, nicknamed him "The Llama." Rijkaard later apologized to Völler, who accepted his apology. Although most soccer players show good sportsmanship, some let their anger get out of control. Over the years, many other spats (so to speak) have taken place during games. Players caught spitting have been fined and banned from the sport for months. When you open your mouth, speak; don't spit!

CHAPTER 10

NO SPIT!

People in different countries have different attitudes about spitting in public. In China and India, it's quite common. Some people in India chew betel nuts and spit out the red juice. In China, many people believe spitting is a way to cleanse the body. Although large cities discourage public spitting and urge people to spit into bins or drains, it's difficult to change an old habit.

In the United States, Canada and most other Western countries, people generally consider spitting in public a disgusting habit (not that people don't do it). But this was not always the case. For centuries, people spat on the floors of their homes, churches, office buildings, buses, trains and toilet cubicles. It was not until medical science discovered that germs cause disease and spittle can carry those germs that customs, attitudes and then laws began to change.

Singapore has one of the strictest no-spitting laws. Spitting in public places can cost up to 1,000 Singapore dollars ($733) for a first offense.

Spitting and Tuberculosis

In the late 1880s, tuberculosis, or TB, was the leading cause of death in the United States, Europe and other parts of the world. The disease, also called consumption and the white plague (because those who suffered from it were so pale), had infected people for thousands of years, but nobody knew what caused it. This changed in 1882 when German doctor and scientist Robert Koch discovered the cause — a bacteria called the tubercle bacillus.

Several years after his discovery, a group of New York City doctors presented a report to the city's health department about how TB might be prevented. The city issued a booklet recommending health measures for citizens. One rule forbid "persons suspected to have consumption to spit on the floor or on cloths unless the latter be immediately burned." This made the connection: saliva could carry sickness, and so public spitting began its downfall.

THOU SHALL NOT SPIT

In 1896 New York passed the first spitting ban in the United States. Europe, too, was beginning to join efforts to prevent the spread of TB. In 1900, the *British Medical Journal* reported that the Vatican was considering how it could help. Some officials in the Catholic Church, including an Italian archbishop, took a stand against spitting on church floors. Anti-spitting notices were posted, and church floors were to be cleaned and disinfected after large group events.

MORE ABOUT ...
Robert Koch

Dr. Robert Koch was a German doctor in the late 1800s and early 1900s. He was one of the founders of microbiology and is known for his research into diseases such as anthrax and cholera. But his claim to fame was his work on tuberculosis — a horrifying disease that had killed one in every seven people up to that point in history. After Koch discovered the tubercle bacillus (the cause of TB) he was able to prove that it was a contagious disease, which helped people focus on preventing its spread. He presented his findings in a famous lecture during which he showed tissue samples from various animals and humans that had died of TB. One scientist in the audience later said the lecture was the most important experience in his scientific life. In 1905 Koch received the Nobel Prize in Medicine for his groundbreaking work on TB. Many thanks, Dr. Koch!

Blame It on the Skirts

In the United States during the early 1900s, spitting bans spread among states, cities and towns. But some groups of men protested the bans as an assault on their right to spit. One medical doctor spoke against the anti-spitting laws and said kissing spread more disease than anything else. He also blamed the spread of disease on women's long skirts (like the one illustrated on this popular magazine of the time). "Ladies' skirts often do the work of the broom," he said, pointing out that they picked up spit from floors, stairs and sidewalks as the women walked. Why should men stop spitting? If women wore shorter skirts and couples stopped kissing, he said, the spread of TB would slow down.

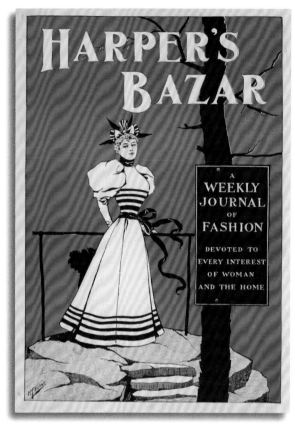

WOMEN TAKE A STAND ON SPIT

Women were outspoken in calling for an end to public spitting. It probably helped that they had the perspective of being non-spitters: they weren't the ones spitting all over the place. (In fact, to this day, most cultures seem to deem it acceptable only for men to spit.) The Women's Health Protective Association, which had chapters in various cities, posted anti-spitting signs on streetcars and steamboats. One sign said, "Spitting in this car is prohibited by law and is punishable by fine of $1 to $5 for each offense." Maybe the fine money went to getting their skirts cleaned?

A NOBLE CALLING

SOME CAME TO CONGRESS TO SERVE THEIR COUNTRY, BUT CORNELIUS
CAME TO USE THE SWEET BRASS SPITTOON.

The Rise of the Spittoon

Not all states banned public spitting. Some, such as Tennessee and Texas, required that railways, businesses and churches provide spittoons (also called cuspidors) — receptacles for people's spit. Through the 1930s and into the 1970s in the Southern states, spittoons were as common as trashcans in public buildings and railway cars. Pubs installed spit troughs beneath the bars. Spittoons came in all shapes, sizes and materials. Most were made of brass, but cheaper ones were made of tin. Doctors told people with TB to use personal pocket spittoons instead of public ones. Metal spittoons were also distributed throughout the Capitol, including a "speaker spittoon" near the rostrum of the Speaker of the House of Representatives in Washington, D.C. But members of Congress didn't always use them. A reporter in 1880 wrote, "your average Congressman often disregards his spittoon and spits on the floor." Even Supreme Court justices had their own cuspidors (at that time there were no women on the court). Today there are eight cuspidors behind the bench, but they are no longer used for spitting. Many years ago, they became wastebaskets. Keeping justice clean!

YOUR OWN PERSONAL SPIT BAG

As Beijing, China, prepared for the 2008 Olympics, city officials wanted to clean up the city for the visitors coming in for the Games. Volunteers handed out "spit bags" and encouraged people to use them instead of spitting in the streets. A year later, the city of Guangzhou decided to crack down. It set up cameras to catch people who spit in public. Anyone caught was fined.

Spit Is in the Eye of the Beholder

So why do people (mostly men) spit in public? It happens all over the world, and different cultures ascribe different meanings to it. But Professor Ross Coomber of the University of Liverpool in the UK wants people to remember that it's all about what you're used to. His field research on spitting in India and China made it clear to him that the judgment of spitting as "dirty" or "gross" was based more on culture than on science — and it was mainly a Western preoccupation. Coomber points out that the claims of spitting-causing disease have been exaggerated. Coughing and sneezing are more likely culprits. Western doctors now tend to agree. According to the Cleveland Clinic, "The risk of transmitting infectious organisms to someone else through saliva is very low. Saliva has antibodies and enzymes that decrease the risk of contagion." Also, people in Western cultures would do well to remember that they too have habits others might find unseemly — such as wearing shoes in the house or blowing their noses in public. Every culture has unique preferences, and that's what makes the world so fascinating.

CHAPTER 11

SPITTING FOR SPORT

People really like to spit. They also love a good competition. Put those things together, and you get spitting contests. Depending on where you live, you can find these contests with watermelon seeds, pumpkin seeds, olive pits, date pits, cherry pits and even crickets. The most unappetizing contests involve spitting antelope and sheep poop — because, yes, anything that goes in your mouth can be spit out. The goal of each contest is to see who can spit the farthest. Hey, it's a way to pass the time!

The record for spitting a cricket is 32 feet and 1/2 inch (9.766 meters). That's almost as long as a telephone pole.

Cricket Spitting

Each spring Purdue University in Lafayette, Indiana, holds a "Bug Bowl." It's one of the largest insect festivals in the world, attracting some 30,000 people who want to learn about bugs. One of the main events is the cricket-spitting contest. Men, women and children compete to see who can spit a cricket the farthest. Contestants compete in one of four categories: senior men, senior women, junior women and junior men. The top-five spitters from each category come back for the championship spit-offs. For the spit-off, each spitter chooses one of three crickets on a silver platter. Very fancy indeed! Though it might sound intriguing, best to talk to your parents before putting a cricket in your ice tray.

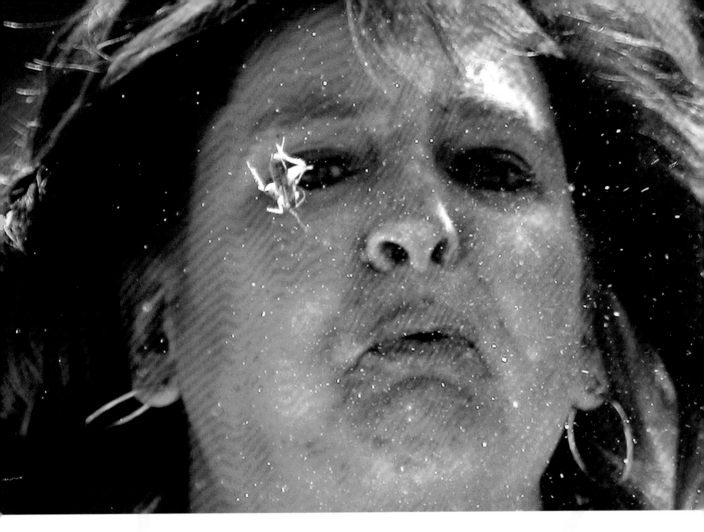

CRICKET SPITTING RULES

To enter the cricket-spitting contest at Purdue's Bug Bowl, you have to follow the rules:

1. Not any old cricket will do. You must use a brown house cricket that has been frozen and slightly thawed for the contest.

2. You must spit the cricket within 20 seconds of putting it in your mouth.

3. You must have the whole cricket in your mouth before stepping into the spitting circle.

4. If you accidentally swallow your cricket, you get one more chance before being disqualified.

5. Before your spit can be counted, an official checks to make sure the cricket still has its 6 legs, 4 wings and 2 antennae. That's in case a contestant accidentally bites off any of the cricket's body parts, which would be cheating (and yucky).

Cherry Spits

Though amateur cherry-spitting competitions have been taking place since the first humans ate this tasty fruit, those wanting something a bit more official are in luck. The Cherry Pit Spit began in 1974 when an American cherry farmer in Eau Claire, Michigan, came up with the idea. It all started as a local gathering, but has since spread to Australia, England, Germany, Ireland and beyond. Now, every year in July, people gather all over the world to challenge each other to a spit-off. The most well known is still the original in Michigan — which is now called the International Cherry Pit–Spitting Championship. As with any good competition, contestants have to follow strict rules. They have 60 seconds to eat a Montmorency cherry and spit the pit. They stand behind the foul line on a platform that overlooks the spitting court. Timekeepers, scorekeepers, pit sweepers and distance judges also participate. This is serious spitting.

WORLD RECORD PIT SPIT

According to *Guinness World Records*, an American man set a new world record when he spat a cherry pit 93 feet and 6 1/2 inches (28.51 meters) in 2004 at the International Cherry Pit–Spitting Championship. That spit is pretty incredible: it's almost as long as an NBA basketball court!

EVERYONE LOSES

BEHIND EVERY DUNG SPITTING CHAMPION IS A SUPPORTIVE
FAMILY WHO WILL NEVER KISS HIM AGAIN.

Did You Say Poop?

People will spit anything. Poop is no exception:

- In South Africa, people — mostly men — compete by spitting dung from the kudu, a type of antelope. Contestants put one of the hard dung pellets in their mouths and spit. The record is 51 feet (just over 15 meters).
- The world's newest dung-spitting contest uses sheep dung. Introduced at a Northern Ireland festival in 2015 to help attract tourists, some 44 men competed to see who could spit the farthest.

Word to the wise: do not try dung spitting at home. It would surely upset your parents . . . and could make you sick.

Spitting Watermelon Seeds

Every year, watermelon seed–spitting contests are held throughout the world. The most famous in the United States is in the small town of Luling, Texas. Every year at a festival called the Watermelon Thump, which has been taking place since 1954, people compete to see who can spit a watermelon seed the farthest. The festival gets its name from the thump sound you hear when you tap a ripe watermelon with your finger. Moms, dads and kids enjoy the fun of spitting the seeds. The record is 68 feet and 9 1/8 inches (almost 21 meters), set in 1989. The winner of each year's competition gets a cash prize, as well as the lifelong honor of knowing they can spit a seed with the best of them.

Spitting Olympics

How far can the sport of spitting go? Maybe an Olympic spit-off one day? Would you participate? Or are you just happy you have enough spit to enjoy your food?
    Ptooey! Ptooey!

ACKNOWLEDGMENTS

The best part of writing a book about a life-sciences subject is making contact with scientists who are doing the real work of advancing knowledge about the topic. Special thanks to Douglas A. Granger, PhD, Chancellor's Professor of Psychology, Public Health, and Pediatrics, Director, Institute for Interdisciplinary Salivary Bioscience Research, University of California, Irvine, who not only shared his own work with me but also opened doors to other researchers. Thanks to Katrine Whiteson, PhD, Assistant Professor, Department of Molecular Biology and Biochemistry, Associate Director, UCI Microbiome Initiative, University of California, Irvine, who introduced me to the world of microbiomes. I am also most grateful to the following, who answered my questions and generously shared their work with me by phone or email: Nancy Dreschel, DVM, PhD, Associate Teaching Professor, Animal Science, Pennsylvania State University; Ivo M.B. Francischetti, MD, PhD, Pathology Resident, Albert Einstein College of Medicine; Michael Gleeson, Emeritus Professor of Exercise Biochemistry, Loughborough University, UK; Charlotte Hacker, Conservation Geneticist; Lance Miller, PhD, Vice President of Conservation Science and Animal Welfare Research, Chicago Zoological Society — Brookfield Zoo; David Pyne, PhD, FACSM, Research Professor, Physiology, Australian Institute of Sport; Kerri Rodriguez, PhD, Student in Human–Animal Interaction, Center for the Human–Animal Bond, Purdue College of Veterinary Medicine; Jack Stewart, Chief Scientific Officer and discoverer of soricidin, Founder of Soricimed Biopharma Inc.; Jennifer Tobey, MA, Researcher, Institute for Conservation Research, San Diego Zoo Global; Jesus G. Valenzuela, PhD, Chief, Vector Molecular Biology Section, Laboratory of Malaria and Vector Research, National Institute of Allergy and Infectious Diseases, NIH; Enno Veerman, Professor, Oral Biochemistry, Academic Centre for Dentistry Amsterdam; David Wong, DMD, DMSc, Professor, Associate Dean for Research, Director for UCLA Center for Oral/Head & Neck Oncology Research, Felix and Mildred Yip Endowed Chair in Dentistry. I thank Steve Cameron, Editorial Director, Firefly Books, and Editor Sarah Howden, who gave this book its final spit and polish, and my agent Barbara Markowitz and Harvey Markowitz for their longtime friendship and support of my work.

PHOTO CREDITS

All illustrations © James Braithwaite unless otherwise credited below.

7T Wellcome Collection; 7B Science Museum, London; 8 Caitlin Rausch; 12B Wikimedia Commons; 15 Wikimedia Commons; 29 John Cancalosi/Alamy; 33 Witthaya Khampanant/Alamy; 41 Gilles Gonthier/Wikimedia Commons; 43 C.O. Mercial/Alamy; 47 Wikimedia Commons; 49 AP Photo/Martina_Hellmann/picture-alliance/dpa/AP Images; 52 Library of Congress: LC-USZC2-5369; 53 Wikimedia Commons; 54 Library of Congress: LC-DIG-ppmsca-42899; 58 AP Photo/The Indianapolis Star, Matt Detrich; 59 AP Photo/The Herald-Palladium, Don Campbell; 61 Tommy Metthe/Abilene Reporter-News via AP

Shutterstock
April_pie (all blobby text boxes); 9 Gillian Santink; 10L Roby 1960; 10M Edwin Butter; 10R Darya Prokapalo; 12T Vikulin; 17 v74; 19 Rocketclips, Inc.; 21 Four Oaks; 22 Teresa Moore; 24 Patrick H; 25 ex0rzist; 26 LouieLea; 28T Huw Penson; 28B Young Swee Ming; 31 reptiles4all; 32T Stuart G Porter; 32B Heiko Kiera; 34 Milan Zygmunt; 35T Ian Dyball; 35B Seregraff; 38T HQuality; 38B Gorodenkoff; 40T Tomasz Klejdysz; 40B Apassara Kanha; 42 Rawpixel.com; 45 Luke Shelley

Cover
Shutterstock: Sebestyen Balint

GLOSSARY

amylase
An enzyme secreted by the salivary glands and pancreas that helps to digest carbohydrates and starches so the body can use them.

autonomic nervous system
The set of nerves that work automatically to regulate internal body functions, such as breathing, heart rate, blood pressure and digestion.

bolus
A ball-like mixture of food and saliva that forms in the mouth when you chew.

catalyst
A substance that speeds up a chemical reaction.

conditioned response
A response that is learned by repeated association with a particular condition, or stimulus, such as the ringing of a bell.

DNA
An abbreviation for deoxyribonucleic acid, a large molecule that contains the instructions for how a living thing will look and function. DNA is in every cell of your body.

expectorating
Another word for spitting.

hemostasis
The stoppage of bleeding.

hormones
Chemical substances secreted by glands. Hormones travel throughout the blood and act as messengers that control the activity of certain cells or organs.

hydrochloric acid
A solution of hydrogen chloride gas (HCL) dissolved in water. This strong acid is produced by the lining of the stomach where it helps to digest food.

immune system
The network of cells, organs and tissues that work together to protect the body against invading viruses and bacteria that cause disease.

microbe
A one-celled organism that can only be seen with a microscope.

opiorphin
A painkilling chemical substance first found in human saliva.

Pavlovian
Relating to the work of Russian scientist Ivan Pavlov, especially his discovery of the conditioned response.

pheromones
Chemical substances secreted externally by some animals, including humans, that influence the behavior of other individuals of the same species. Pheromones are released by urine and skin. They are detected by smell and are used to mark territory, signal readiness to mate, or communicate an alarm.

physiologist
A biologist who studies the functioning of living organisms.

placebo
A fake treatment, such as a sugar pill, that is used in clinical studies to help researchers as a comparison against the effect of a new drug. Study participants don't know whether they are receiving the drug or the placebo. Sometimes the placebo has a beneficial effect because the people taking it believe they are getting the real drug and expect it will help them. What a person thinks or believes can affect their health. Doctors call this the "placebo effect."

plaque
A slimy coating containing bacteria that forms on the teeth and can cause cavities. A different kind of plaque can form in the arteries and cause heart disease and stroke.

post-traumatic stress disorder (PTSD)
A mental health problem caused by experiencing a terrifying event such as war or a school shooting. People of any age can develop PTSD.

proboscis
A long, flexible snout such as the trunk of an elephant or the tubular organ that insects use for sucking or piercing.

spittoon
A receptacle for spit.

vaccine
A substance injected into the body that increases immunity to a particular infectious disease, such as measles, and prevents its spread. Vaccines have saved millions of people's lives from once fatal diseases such as smallpox and diphtheria.

INDEX

Words in **bold** mean they are in the glossary on page 63.
Page numbers in *italics* mean there is a picture on that page.